ILONA MAHER BIOGRAPHY: A RUGBY ICON

LUKE C. CASEY

All rights reserved. No part of this publication may be reproduced, distributed, or transmitted in any form or by any means, including photocopying, recording, and other electronic or mechanical methods, without prior written permission of the publisher, except in case of briefs quotation embodied in critical reviews and certain other noncommercial uses permitted by copyright law.

Copyright © LUKE C. CASEY, 2025.

TABLE OF CONTENTS

INTRODUCTION

CHAPTER ONE: EARLY DAYS

CHAPTER TWO: THE ROAD TO RUGBY

CHAPTER THREE: RISING THROUGH THE RANKS

CHAPTER FOUR: ON THE WORLD STAGE

CHAPTER FIVE: BEYOND THE FIELD

CHAPTER SIX: LESSONS FROM ILONA

CHAPTER SEVEN: ILONA MAHER'S EVOLVING LEGACY

CHAPTER EIGHT: LOOKING AHEAD

CONCLUSION

FUN FACTS ABOUT ILONA MAHER

INTRODUCTION

Ilona Maher is more than just a rugby player. She's a wild force, a role model for young players everywhere, and a shining example of what it means to follow your dreams. Ilona's story goes from her humble roots in Burlington, Vermont, to the big stage of the Olympics. It's a story of determination, resilience, and a strong belief in herself.

People look up to Ilona because she is brave, has great skill, and can connect with fans anywhere. She is a role model for anyone who wants to dream big. It wasn't easy for her to become famous. Ilona faced every challenge head-on, whether it was switching sports in college or working out nonstop to fight on the world stage. She showed that determination and a positive outlook can get you past even the toughest problems.

But Ilona is more than what she has done in rugby. We should laugh, enjoy life, and not take ourselves too seriously because of her. Through her social media posts, she's shown that athletes can inspire people not only with their skills, but also by being real and kind.

The path of Ilona Maher's life is told in this book, which is a celebration of her life. This story is for people who want to reach for the stars, even if the way there isn't always clear. Ilona's story will captivate and inspire you, whether you're a rugby fan, a hopeful athlete, or just someone looking for a good read.

Welcome to the life of a true rugby icon, someone who shows us every day that anything is possible if we work hard and have guts. Welcome to Ilona Maher's amazing trip!

CHAPTER ONE: EARLY DAYS

Ilona Maher's story starts in Burlington, Vermont, a beautiful city known for its small-town feel and close-knit community. Born into a loving and caring family, Ilona grew up in a place that encouraged her to be curious and competitive. From a very young age, her parents, Michael and Patty Maher, taught her the importance of working hard, being kind, and not giving up. These ideas would help her be successful in sports and in life in general.

Ilona learned quickly how to work with others and compete as the youngest of three siblings. Her house was always laughing, arguing, and playing games, which made it a great place for a young athlete to grow. She had a natural interest in sports from a very young age. Every time Ilona played school games or raced her brothers in the backyard, her boundless energy and enthusiasm were hard to miss.

Ilona had lots of chances to explore the woods when she was growing up in Vermont. She loved hiking on trails, swimming in clear lakes, and riding her bike through quiet streets in the summer. In the winter, people went sledding, skiing, and had ice fights. She stayed physically fit by doing these things, and they also helped her grow a deep love for nature and adventure.

Ilona was more than just a sports star in school. Because she was so lively, she was naturally in charge of her friends. Her humor and unwavering drive made her teachers and classmates look up to her. But her road to becoming a great rugby player wasn't easy. Even as a kid, Ilona had no idea that she would one day love rugby so much. Instead, she tried many sports, such as soccer, basketball, and field hockey, and did well in all of them. This made her very versatile as an athlete.

Ilona really shone in field hockey more than any other event. She worked hard at improving her skills for a long time, often practicing after her friends had gone home. She quickly became known as a star player because she was always trying to get better and got along well with others. Yet, even though Ilona was good at field hockey, she felt drawn to something else, something that would let her use all of her strength, speed, and competitive energy.

During these growing years, family was very important. She wanted to do better because her father, Michael, was an athlete and told her stories of how he kept going even when things got hard. Her mother, Patty, was her biggest fan and always told her to stay grounded and smile through every struggle. Her parents raised her in a home where goals were encouraged and mistakes were seen as opportunities to learn and grow.

Ilona had problems like any other child, even though she was gifted and had a good family life. It wasn't always easy to balance sports, schoolwork, and friendships. She had times when she was confused and angry, but her family and friends were always there for her. These events taught her to be strong, which was very important as she went through the ups and downs of her sports career.

By the time Ilona started high school, it was clear that she had a lot of athletic ability. Coaches and teammates praised how hard she worked and how she could inspire others. She kept getting better at field hockey, but she also tried basketball, which helped her improve her balance and ability to think strategically. Even though she didn't know it yet, these skills would come in handy when she first played rugby.

During Ilona's childhood, she learned new things, grew, and got ambitious. She got from Burlington to the world stage by taking small, determined steps. Her loving family, a strong sense of who she was, and her unwavering desire to be the best helped her along the way. These early years were not only the start of her story, but also the base on which her amazing life was built.

CHAPTER TWO: THE ROAD TO RUGBY

It wasn't easy for Ilona Maher to get into rugby. She hadn't even thought about rugby when she was just starting out as an athlete. Traditional sports like field hockey and basketball came naturally to her. Her strength, speed, and ability to think strategically made her the best on the courts and fields. Still, Ilona felt like something was missing, even though she was doing well. She was looking for a sport that would push her in new ways and let her show off her competitive spirit and physical strength.

For Ilona, rugby didn't really start until she went to college. She went to Connecticut's Quinnipiac University and originally kept focusing on field hockey there. But as luck would have it, she soon found herself pulled to a new chance that would make her life different forever. The Quinnipiac women's rugby team was growing, and the coach was looking for players who could give the team strength, speed, and flexibility. They were impressed by Ilona's athletic past and desire to win, which caught their attention.

Ilona was interested but hesitant when she was first asked to join the rugby team. She wasn't very good at rugby, and the thought of switching to something she didn't know much about was scary. But because she liked difficulties, she chose to give it a shot. Once Ilona set foot on a rugby field, she knew she had found her calling. She was looking for a game that was fast, exciting, and physical, and this one was it.

It wasn't easy to learn how to play rugby properly. Ilona had to learn new skills, tactics, and even words. She had no idea how to pass the ball backwards, scrummage, or tackle, but she took on these new skills with the same drive she had put into everything else in her life. She studied the game for hours, watched professional games, and asked her coaches and peers for help. With time and effort, she learned the rules of the game and how to best use her natural agility.

Ilona had a hard time getting used to how physically demanding rugby was. A very high level of strength, endurance, and toughness was needed for the sport. She was strong before rugby, but it made her stronger. She trained hard both on and off the field, getting the strength and endurance she needed to play at a high level. She learned to respect her body and what it could do along the way.

While playing rugby, Ilona improved very quickly and well. She quickly stood out on the Quinnipiac team and helped them win several national titles. Because she could read the game, run hard, and hit without fear, she was an important part of the team. She also brought a lot of energy and drive to the team, which made everyone else want to work harder.

Ilona began to dream bigger as she went through college. She learned that rugby was more than just a college sport; it was a worldwide event with high-level competitions. USA Rugby scouts were impressed by how well she played at Quinnipiac, and soon she was asked to train with the national team. It both excited and scared Ilona to think about representing her country, but she was ready to take on the task.

A big turning point in Ilona's career was when she joined the USA Women's Rugby team. It was the first step in her journey from being an athlete in college to a competitive rugby player. There was a whole new level of focus when she trained with the national team. Even though the other players were faster, bigger, and had more experience, Ilona was determined to show them who was boss. She worked on her skills for hours on end, learning from her friends and trying to be the best she could be.

Ilona had difficulties and times of doubt during this time. There were days when she thought the training was too hard or when she wondered if she was up to the challenges of international rugby. Yet, every time she thought about giving up, she remembered why she had begun. She wasn't going to give up rugby because it gave her a sense of purpose and connection.

What Ilona did to get into rugby showed how strong, flexible, and determined she was. She didn't have an easy journey, but it made her the athlete and person she is now. Ilona found her passion by moving out of her comfort zone and embracing the unknown. This passion would take her to the world stage and beyond. She wasn't just looking for a sport on her way to rugby; she was also looking for herself.

CHAPTER THREE: RISING THROUGH THE RANKS

As soon as Ilona Maher got good at rugby, her career took a very different path. Her love for the sport, along with her unwavering drive and hard work ethic, helped her go from being a potential college player to a rising star on the world stage. But the journey was not easy. She had to be very dedicated, have a lot of mental and physical endurance, and have a strong confidence in her ability to succeed.

USA Rugby took notice of Ilona's skills after she did well at Quinnipiac University and helped her college team win national titles. Going from college rugby to the national team was a big step up, and Ilona had to deal with new difficulties at this high level of competition. There were seasoned professionals in the USA Rugby team. Many of them had played rugby their whole lives. Since Ilona got into the sport later than most of them, she had to work very hard to show that she belonged with them.

It was hard work to train with the national team. A lot of the time, players were pushed to their mental and physical limits during practices. Ilona's days were full of tactical lessons, team-building activities, and conditioning drills that didn't leave much time for anything else. But instead of being stressed out, she did well in this high-pressure setting. She was driven by the task of playing with and against some of the best players in the country. She looked at what her opponents did, worked on her skills, and asked her coaches for comments. She was always trying to get better.

Ilona's ability to change was one of her best qualities. Ilona was great at all three parts of rugby: speed, strength, and planning. Her time playing field hockey, basketball, and other sports had given her a unique view on how to move and be aware of the game. She quickly became known for her strong runs, quick thinking, and power to read the game. These things about her made her stand out and made her an important part of the team.

When Ilona first went on the national stage, she was both excited and nervous. It was an honor and a duty to wear the USA jersey, and she went into every game with a clear sense of what she wanted to achieve. There was a lot of competition, and each foreign team brought their own style and strategy to the game. Ilona, on the other hand, stepped up to the challenge and gave shows that showed off her skills. She learned something new from every match and used what she learned to improve her game.

Ilona's confidence grew as she got more experience. She became more sure of herself as a leader and a player, both on and off the field. Her positive energy and enthusiasm made her a fan favorite as well as a partner. Whether it was telling a joke to lighten the mood during a tough practice or getting up to inspire the team during a game, she wasn't afraid to be herself. Being real became one of the things that made her stand out, making her a favorite among her fans and an inspiration to budding athletes.

It wasn't easy for her to move up the ranks. Getting hurt, which is a normal part of being an athlete, tried her strength. While she was getting better, she sometimes had to watch her friends play from the sidelines. These times were hard, but Ilona wouldn't let them define who she was. She studied rugby tactics and kept in touch with her team to work on her mental game. Every failure made her more determined to come back stronger.

Ilona worked hard, and it paid off when she started getting more playing time and attention on the world stage. She competed for the US against the best teams in the world in prestigious competitions. When she played, she was electric because she could break through defenders and set up goals for her team. Each match she played made it clear that she was one of the sport's growing stars.

In addition to her success on the field, Ilona loved being a rugby champion. She knew how important it was to spark the imaginations of young people, especially girls who might not see themselves portrayed in games like rugby. She talked about her trip on social media, at community events, and in public, inspiring others to dream big and work hard to reach their targets.

In Ilona Maher's life, rising through the ranks of rugby changed everything. It was an era of progress, finding, and unwavering dedication to doing the best. She showed that anyone can overcome any challenge and become great if they are determined, flexible, and have faith in themselves. Ilona went from being a newbie to becoming a key player on the national team. This showed how dedicated and characterful she was and set the stage for even bigger and better things to come.

CHAPTER FOUR: ON THE WORLD STAGE

Taking the world stage was a dream come true for Ilona Maher and the best way to see how good she really was. It marked the moment when she went from being a rising star in American rugby to a player known all over the world. When she started competing at the international level, she faced new difficulties, had higher expectations, and had chances to show off her skills that she had never had before. The best performers could do well on that stage, and Ilona was keen to make her mark.

When Ilona played for the US in a big international tournament for the first time, it felt like a dream. She knew what it meant to wear the USA shirt; it was the result of years of hard work, sacrifice, and determination. As she stood on the field with her teammates and listened to the national song, she felt a strong sense of duty and pride. It wasn't just for fun; she was playing for her country, her team, and everyone who had helped her get here.

Rugby on the international level was a whole other animal. Ilona had never seen the game move faster, the competition tougher, or the stakes higher than they were. Teams from New Zealand, England, and Australia, which have played rugby for a long time, brought a level of skill and plan that needed to be changed all the time. To compete at this level, Ilona knew she had to step up her game, and she took on the task with the determination that she always shows.

Her big start on the world stage was nothing less than amazing. It didn't take long for both critics and fans to notice how athletic and versatile Ilona was. She was very good at getting through defenses by using her strength and speed to win valuable meters for her team. Ilona's presence on the field was electrifying, whether she was making a hard hit, throwing a precise pass, or leading a counterattack.

A lot of people around the world liked Ilona because she was charming and real. She became famous for both her acts and the honest and funny way she was. She shared behind-the-scenes looks of her life as a world rugby player on social media sites like TikTok and Instagram, which helped her become more well-known. People all over the world connected with her funny and positive posts, which brought women's rugby to a new level of attention.

There were some tough parts to competing on the world stage. International events were very hard on both the body and the mind. Ilona had to get used to new time zones and move across continents to play against some of the toughest teams in the sport. There was steady pressure to do well, and there wasn't much room for error. However, Ilona's strength and mental toughness helped her do well in these situations. No matter what happened, she saw every match as a chance to learn and grow.

During a big global tournament, Ilona's international career reached a turning point when the USA Women's Rugby team played some of the best teams in the world. Ilona was a key part of the team's success, putting on amazing shows that showed off her skill, drive, and ability to lead. Her coaches, coworkers, and fans all praised her for being able to step up when things got tough.

Ilona learned more about the sport and its global community while she was on the world stage. She became friends with people from other countries and learned about their ways of life and points of view. These conversations made her experience better and made her more sure that rugby is a sport that can be played by people from all over the world.

Ilona also took her job as a world ambassador for rugby very seriously when she wasn't playing. Using her fame to push for more attention and support for women's sports, she stressed how important it is to be fair and represented. A lot of young athletes, mostly girls, were inspired by her work to play rugby and dream of competing at the top levels.

For Ilona Maher, being on the world stage meant more than just winning matches. It meant embracing the honor and duty of serving something bigger than herself. She led the way for her team, her country, and rugby, showing how the sport can bring people together and inspire them. It was Ilona's time on the world stage that solidified her reputation as a leader and an inspiration. She showed the world that desire, hard work, and being yourself can have a lasting effect.

CHAPTER FIVE: BEYOND THE FIELD

Ilona Maher did amazing things on the rugby field, but her influence went far beyond the sporting world. Off the field, she was a force for good, advocacy, and connection. She used her fame to motivate others, support important causes, and change the idea of what it meant to be an athlete in the 21st century.

The first thing that drove Ilona to leave the field was her desire to be herself in public. Because she was a skilled athlete, she knew how much power she had and chose to use it for good. She became known as a personable and approachable figure through social media, public events, and work in the community.

Her use of social media became an important part of who she was outside of baseball. There were places for Ilona to meet with her fans that felt real and unplanned, like

TikTok and Instagram. She posted funny videos, honest thoughts, and short clips from her life as a professional rugby player. These gave people a look behind the scenes at a world they didn't know much about. Because she could be funny and honest at the same time, she became famous on the internet and brought attention to women's rugby in ways that traditional media often missed.

Ilona's comedy, on the other hand, always had something serious behind it. She used her fame to talk about important topics, like the problems women face in sports, the value of mental health, and the need for more support and attention for women's rugby. Her audience really connected with these messages and admired her courage in speaking out and her willingness to talk about tough subjects.

Fighting for mental health became one of Ilona's main interests. She knew how hard it could be on an athlete's mental health because she had been through the ups and downs of professional sports. Ilona talked about how she dealt with anxiety and the pressures of success, which broke down the stereotypes about mental health in sports. Others were more likely to ask for help because she was honest, which helped build a culture of support and understanding in the rugby community and beyond.

Ilona's dedication to guiding the next generation was another important part of her life outside of rugby. She often went to schools, community centers, and youth rugby groups to tell kids her story and encourage them to follow their dreams. Ilona's lesson was simple but powerful: if you work hard, are honest, and believe in yourself, you can do amazing things.

Her job as a mentor went beyond just showing up in public. Ilona worked with groups that wanted to promote gender equality in sports and give people in neglected areas more access to rugby. She thought that sports could change people, not just as a way to stay fit, but also as a way to boost confidence, resilience, and a sense of connection.

As her power grew, so did her chances to make a change. Ilona started working with brands and sponsors that shared her values. She used these partnerships to bring attention to issues that were important to her. Ilona made sure that the things she backed had a deeper meaning, like backing women-led projects, promoting sustainable practices, or fighting for mental health resources.

Ilona made time for the simple things in life that kept her grounded, even though she had a lot going on. She talked a lot about how important it was to keep her personal and work lives in balance. Ilona stressed how important it was to put one's health first, whether it was by spending time with family, trying out new hobbies, or just taking a moment to relax.

It was one of Ilona's best qualities that she could connect with people on a personal level. Fans, teammates, and coworkers all said she made others feel seen and important. She treated everyone she met with kindness and sincerity, and that made an impact on everyone.

Ilona Maher's life outside of sports showed what kind of person she was and how determined she was to make a difference. She knew that her memory would be made up of more than just her rugby accomplishments. It would also include how she helped others and used her fame for good. Ilona became more than just a rugby star because of how funny, honest, and passionate she was. She became an inspiration to everyone who wants to make a change in their own way.

CHAPTER SIX: LESSONS FROM ILONA

Going through Ilona Maher's life, on and off the rugby field, has taught me many things that are not just about sports. Her story isn't just about how well she did in sports; it's also about being strong, being real, and having the guts to be yourself. Ilona has taught those who follow her journey a lot of useful things through her actions and words.

Ilona's life shows us how important it is to keep going even when things get hard. Ilona faced many problems along the way, from her early years as a multi-sport athlete to her rise to fame as an international rugby star. These problems could have stopped her from going after her goals. Ilona was always determined to get past problems, even when there weren't enough resources for women's rugby or when training was hard on her body or when she had to compete on a world stage. Her story shows how important it is to keep working toward your goals, even when things get hard.

Ilona's focus on self-belief is also very uplifting. People don't always believe that women can do well in sports, but Ilona forged her own path with conviction and confidence. She wouldn't let stereotypes or societal standards hold her back. She instead accepted her unique skills and made the most of them. We can learn from her story that faith in ourselves is the first thing that needs to be done to reach greatness.

Being honest is what makes Ilona unique, and it's also one of the most important things she can teach. Sometimes, social media shows perfect people, but Ilona has decided to show the world who she really is. People from all walks of life can relate to her because she is funny, open, and honest. By what she does, she shows us that it's okay to make mistakes, laugh at ourselves, and talk about our problems. She shows us that being honest is not a problem but a strength that helps people connect with each other in a real way.

Another thing we can learn from Ilona's story is how important it is to use our power for good. As her fame grew, she became aware of the duty that came with it. Ilona stopped focusing only on her own success and became a strong voice for causes she cared about, such as mental health and equal rights for women in sports. Her deeds show how important it is to care about others and try to make the world a better place.

The story of Ilona's journey also shows how important society and working together are. Because rugby is a team sport, it taught her how important it is to trust and help her peers. Inside and outside of sports, Ilona showed her friends, peers, and young athletes who looked up to her the same sense of community. She believed in helping others and making a place where everyone could do well. Her method reminds us that most of the time, success doesn't happen by itself; it takes the work of a group and the support of a community.

Ilona's fight for mental health is one of the most moving lessons from her story. She has helped remove the shame surrounding mental health problems by being open about her own battles with anxiety and the stress of competitive sports. People are more likely to put their own health first and get help when they need it because Ilona is honest. Her message is clear: taking care of your mental health is a sign of power, not weakness, and it's just as important as your physical health.

We can also learn from Ilona to enjoy the trip. Even though her job was very demanding, she never forgot how important it was to have fun and stay connected to the things she loved. Ilona showed us that life isn't just about getting to the finish line; it's also about enjoying the little things along the way, like sharing a funny TikTok video or laughing with her friends.

Finally, Ilona's narrative shows us how important it is to have big dreams. Even though she came from a small town, she showed the world that no dream is too big for people who are willing to work hard for it. Her success is an inspiration to everyone who is brave enough to go after their goals, no matter how far away they may seem.

Ilona Maher left behind a tradition of strength, honesty, and unwavering hope. Her actions have shown us that what makes someone great is not just what they accomplish, but also how they affect others and the lessons they leave behind. Her story shows that we can make a worthwhile and inspiring life for ourselves if we accept ourselves as we are, work hard, and help others as we rise.

CHAPTER SEVEN: ILONA MAHER'S EVOLVING LEGACY

Ilona Maher is still making a name for herself in rugby, but her story has taken some new and exciting turns that show not only how good she is at sports but also how much she affects culture and sports in general. Ilona's life has changed a lot in 2024. She is trying new things that are changing the way people think about women's sports.

Maher switched her focus from rugby sevens to rugby union in December 2024. She signed a short-term deal with the Bristol Bears, a well-known team in England's Premiership Women's Rugby. This change was a big one for her career because it meant she moved from playing fast-paced sevens rugby to playing more precise and physical rugby union. By switching teams and formats, she not only improved her chances of making the US Women's Eagles Rugby World Cup team for the 2025 event, but she also made the move with a plan. Ilona has always been determined to represent her country on the world stage, and her new job with the Bears shows how hard she works to be the best.

Her signing has effects that go far beyond her skills on the game. Not only is Ilona a very good athlete, but she is also very active on social media, which she has used for a long time to push for change in women's rugby. Ilona has built a following of millions of people on social media sites like Instagram and TikTok, which is not just rugby fans. A lot of people, not just sports fans, know her name because of her funny and understandable posts. Her new deal with the Bristol Bears fits right in with the growing trend of players using their fame to bring more attention to their sport. Because the Bears know how influential Ilona is, they have hired a social media manager to help promote women's rugby and get more people to watch it. Without a question, Ilona's support will help the sport break down barriers and gain new fans, especially younger people who may not have played rugby before.

It's clear that Ilona sees her stage as more than just a way to show off her skills; she sees it as a way to make the sport she loves better. Her work to make rugby easier to get into and more popular will surely inspire new players and get more young women interested in the sport. Ilona is a key person in the fight for gender equality in sports because she is both a great athlete and a social media whiz. This is important because women's sports are often underfunded and underappreciated.

Ilona's power doesn't just come from rugby fields and social media. She has used her fame to support many causes, especially mental health and how important it is to take care of yourself. Ilona has been open about the problems she faces as a professional athlete. This shows how many athletes deal with mental and emotional problems. She also speaks out about how important it is to keep skincare and self-care practices simple. She supports natural and simple ways to look beautiful. She believes in taking a simple, no-nonsense approach to health and fitness, which shows in her skin care routine, which focuses on keeping her skin hydrated and using peptides. Ilona doesn't just talk about taking care of your body; she also tells her fans to do things that will help them keep their mental and emotional health in a world that is getting faster and faster.

Ilona's skills and hobbies have grown beyond rugby to include entertainment. As of November 2024, she had been on the popular TV show "Dancing with the Stars," where she showed a different side of herself. When Ilona danced with experienced dancer Alan Bersten, the crowd was captivated by her natural charm and dancing skills, and she came in second place in the competition. This experience showed Ilona's public image a new side. It showed how flexible she was and how ready she was to take on challenges outside of her comfort zone. It also showed how well she could connect with people in different entertainment industries.

She showed how versatile she is and how determined she is to do well in everything she sets her mind to by competing on "Dancing with the Stars." Whatever she does, Ilona Maher shows that she can do anything. She has done this on the rugby field, on a national TV show, and as a fighter for women's sports.

Ilona's future looks like it will be full of opportunities. She has a huge amount of ability to keep making a difference on and off the field. No matter what she does in her rugby career, she will always be an important part of the growth of women's rugby in the US and around the world. But she also wants to do things outside of sports. She is becoming more visible in entertainment and the media, so we don't know where her impact will take her next. She might host more TV shows, fight for women's rights, or use her social media to bring attention to issues that are important to her.

The memory of Ilona Maher is changing all the time. She is a great example of what it means to push limits, take advantage of new chances, and stay true to yourself. She went from being a great rugby player to a dynamic and multifaceted public figure. Ilona keeps changing what it means to be an athlete, a role model, and a woman who is shaping the future of culture and sports with each new project. No matter how many years pass, Ilona Maher will always be able to break down walls, inspire others, and leave her mark on everything she does.

CHAPTER EIGHT: LOOKING AHEAD

Ilona Maher's amazing career has come to a crossroads. The future is full of opportunities as big and exciting as her journey so far. Ilona's achievements in rugby have made her one of the sport's biggest stars, but her goals and dreams go far beyond the field. She is determined, funny, and passionate, and she looks forward to a future that will be just as important as her past.

Ilona's continued involvement in rugby is both a rock that keeps things stable and a source of inspiration for the sport. She has been fighting on the world stage for years and is still an important part of her team. She brings a mix of skill, leadership, and guidance that makes those around her better. Ilona's dedication to getting better at what she does means that she will stay a strong player in international rugby for many years to come. Her unwavering commitment to the sport she loves shows in her desire to help the US reach new heights in women's rugby.

Ilona's impact, on the other hand, is not limited to how well she plays the field. She has already become a strong supporter of women's rugby, and I'm sure she will do even more to promote the sport in the years to come. Ilona keeps raising awareness of women's rugby by giving speeches, working with rugby groups, and having a bigger and bigger social media presence. She does this by challenging old ideas and pushing for more support and respect.

Ilona is in a great situation to inspire the next generation of athletes because she is a role model. Her relationship with young players has always been an important part of her legacy, and she is still very dedicated to helping rugby grow at the local level. Ilona inspires young players to believe that they can also do great things by going to schools, holding clinics, and telling their stories. Her goal is to make rugby easier for people in communities that haven't had many sports options in the past. This will have an effect on people from all walks of life and income levels.

Ilona is making a name for herself as a public person with many sides besides her athletic career. Her talent for sharing stories and her ability to connect with people from all walks of life have given her chances to work in media, entertainment, and advocacy. Ilona's social media accounts used to show bits of her life as an athlete, but now they're powerful ways for her to spread important messages and connect with her fans in deep ways.

It looks like Ilona will probably get more involved with the media at some point. Her sense of humor, ability to connect with people, and natural charm make her a great choice for commentating, broadcasting, or even having her own show. These kinds of activities would help her spread the sport of rugby to more people while showing off her friendly nature and deep understanding.

Giving to others is another option Ilona could look into. Because she cares so much about mental health, equal rights for women, and building communities, she might be able to lead projects that have a long impact. Ilona is likely to put her energy into causes that are very important to her, whether she does this by starting her own foundation or working with already existing groups.

Aside from her work goals, Ilona also has personal goals for the future. She wants to live a life that includes both goals and happiness because she has talked a lot about how important balance is. Spending time with family and friends, exploring new places, and pursuing creative hobbies are just a few of Ilona's ways that she wants to live a full and meaningful life.

It's still not clear what Ilona will do, but one thing is for sure, her journey is far from over. She will continue to do well no matter what obstacles or chances come her way because she is strong, has a clear vision, and can adapt. Ilona Maher is more than just an athlete. She is a leader, a speaker, and a change agent. As she looks ahead, her story serves as a lesson that greatness is not a goal, but a journey that must be driven by passion, purpose, and a strong desire to make a difference.

In the years to come, Ilona's impact will definitely spread, changing lives, breaking down obstacles, and leaving a mark on the world that will never be erased. People can learn from her story to think big, take on challenges, and look forward to the future with hope and determination. Ilona Maher will definitely face whatever comes her way with the same bold, honest, and unstoppable spirit that has shaped her life so far.

CONCLUSION

Ilona Maher's story shows how powerful desire, toughness, and a never-ending drive to be the best can be. Before she became a global rugby star, Ilona grew up in Vermont. She has changed not only what it means to be an athlete, but also what it means to be a leader, a role model, and a trailblazer in the modern world.

She switched from rugby sevens to rugby union with the Bristol Bears, which is just one example of how she is always trying to push the limits of her sport. Ilona has shown over and over that her impact goes far beyond her athletic skills, whether she's making history on the field or using her fame to improve women's rugby. Ilona has become a voice for change on social media, with millions of followers. She has helped make women's sports more well-known and is inspiring a new generation to think big and go after their goals.

Ilona's story is about more than just rugby, though. It's about taking advantage of new chances, leaving your comfort zone, and always changing. Her time on "Dancing with the Stars" proved that she isn't afraid to try new things, showing that success doesn't have to happen in just one area. Ilona has used her fame to make a difference in areas other than rugby. She has spoken out for mental health, made skincare practices easier, and shared her own experiences with the world.

When we look to the future, Ilona Maher's influence is just getting started. As long as she keeps making waves in rugby, entertainment, and lobbying, she will definitely inspire a lot of people to follow their own paths, no matter how strange or difficult they may seem. She left behind a story of bravery, strength, and an unwavering spirit that doesn't let limits define her.

Ilona's story shows that being great isn't just about awards or victories, but also about having the guts to take on new challenges, help others along the way, and leave an effect that lasts for generations. The world can't wait to see what she does next on her journey.

FUN FACTS ABOUT ILONA MAHER

Ilona Maher has a lot of interesting and fun things about her life besides her rugby achievements. One of the most interesting things about her is how she can combine being sporty with being funny and relatable. Ilona is a professional athlete, but she is also known for having a lively attitude and a lot of energy that makes her stand out both on and off the field.

It's no secret that Ilona is fun and interesting on social media, where she shares behind-the-scenes moments with her fans. From funny dares to weird dance moves, her Instagram and TikTok pages are full of fun videos that show off her playful side. It's amazing how she can make her fans laugh and feel like they know her. This shows that athletes don't have to be serious all the time to be admired. Outside of acting, she has a great sense of humor that makes people laugh all the time, even in the most serious sports settings.

Fans love to learn about fun facts about Ilona, like how much she loves to travel. As a professional rugby player, she's been to some of the most exciting places in the world for training camps and competitions. It's clear that she loves to travel, and she's not afraid to share pictures and movies from her trips. Without fail, Ilona takes every chance to see the world, whether it's by visiting new places or trying new foods. She also keeps her fans up to date on her travels.

Beyond her love of traveling, Ilona also loves to keep things easy. Even though she has a famous job, she supports a simple approach to beauty and face care. She keeps it simple with her skincare routine, which focuses on self-care and keeping her skin hydrated, which many of her fans like. She lives her life by the simple idea of "stay grounded, stay true to yourself, and enjoy the journey."

Ilona is a star in entertainment fields other than rugby and social media. She showed this on "Dancing with the Stars," where her surprising dance moves and charm wowed viewers. This sudden change into a field other than rugby added to her already impressive personality and showed that she can do well in any area she chooses to study.

Ilona also really wants women to have power and men and women to have similar rights. She always uses her fame to talk about how important it is to support women's sports by telling stories about the struggles and successes of female athletes. By what she does and says, she helps make the world a better place for young girls to be inspired to follow their dreams, no matter what those dreams are.

One of the best things about Ilona Maher is that she is honest. She is herself and doesn't try to be someone else. She's honest, friendly, and easy to get in touch with, which helps fans of all ages connect with her even more. It's clear that she is herself in everything she does, from playing rugby to posting a funny video on social media to talking about health issues. People love Ilona Maher because she is funny, relatable, and strong. She is well-known in sports and beyond.

With her drive and determination along with her love of having fun, Ilona is a great role model who is both inspiring and entertaining.

Made in the USA
Columbia, SC
22 January 2025